OnWard

Tell the truth; shame the devil.

You keep saying you want to have something different—but you are not doing something different to have what you say you want.

That's called lying to yourself. Trust me. I know.

I did it for years and wondered why people with zero talent were making BIG $$$ and I was just making ends meet. WITH MY BUSINESS, CAREER even my CREDIT! Until one day, I did something that changed my life.

It's so embarrassing and raw, I doubt if you will believe me. But here it goes...

I got into a "street fight" with myself—on my OWN behalf!

I'm serious. I had to get into a metaphysical bare-knuckle brawl with myself about my value... to me.

It was a bloody fight. I realized I was STILL blaming "Momma and 'em," White people, old lovers—everyone. I was victimizing myself. And if I wanted something different for me, I had to take me on and invest in myself. I don't just mean the money. The money is the EASY part! I had to be willing to value me instead of begging other motherfuckers to validate me with scraps of tenderness, love, and pennies on the dollar.

And once I took me on, life changed. My behaviors changed. I put myself in rooms with people and mentors who were going places

I craved instead of dragging the dead weight on my back from the people who had hurt me.

Here's the thing: **if you want something different, you have to do something different**. If you want to have what have, you have to do what other successful people do. If you want to get on the path to success, then get in the room with a other successes and learn. Education is the panacea for all i-don't-know-isms, ignorance, enslaved mindset, and plain stupidity.

What's the holdup?

We can have a million excuses and we can even solicit excuses from other people (staying enslaved) but it still won't amount to nothing. I did it, until I was tired of being in the black hole of discouragement. The vast majority will always have excuses for why your career didn't take off and why this house didn't work out but excuses are not made UNLESS you never tried. YOU like me will get the money to do what we WANT or DESIRE to soothe our (ego). So why not invest the time in you, build up your self-respect, self-esteem and improve your life.

Edna J. White

The Psychology of Buying a Home I'm so
honored and excited to be part of your transition from renting to homeownership. SEARCHING, evaluating, contemplating ... maybe even procrastinating. These are things we have all been confronted with when buying a house. Yet there are other forces that can be at work while making one of the biggest decisions we are likely to make. So much emotion, calculation and imagination can go into it.

Buying a house is a big deal, and everyone involved in the process knows that. Most of us spend months researching, evaluating, or choosing the most suitable neighbourhood before we are able to make a well-informed decision to purchase. We tend to think that we are completely rational about the buying process; however, the opposite is often true, and there are many more subtle processes going on. Ignoring these important nuances might have a great impact on your final choice. Even if you do not openly follow your inner urges and choose your dream home according to your lucky house number, we naturally stray from the path of clear-headedness when we face such an important decision. Let's take a closer look at the psychology of home-buying to learn more about the hidden details that can influence our decisions.

Have you ever thought about the **Psychology of Buying a Home**? Maybe you haven't really thought about it, or that there may be a such a thing, but there is. The entire mental and emotional process of buying a home, of thinking about all the issues that buying a home entails, of negotiating the price and terms, and of being in an adversarial relationship with a seller when so much is at stake–all of this involves a dynamic exchange of conscious and subconscious thoughts during the process of buying a home.

Most buyers are unaware of the importance of understanding the
.

Buying your first home is not something you (or anyone) should take lightly. You should be prepared with as much information about the process as you can learn before you begin. You should understand your real estate market and the current mortgage market. The more you know – the better.

Maybe the stories of two buyers will open the secret hinged barriers to your own mental and emotional world and to your own psychology of buying a home. H.G. Wells, "We should strive to welcome change and challenges, because they are what help us grow. Without them we grow weak like the Eloi in comfort and security. We need to constantly be challenging ourselves in order to strengthen our character and increase our intelligence. " Hats off to progress!

The Psychology of Buying a Home – Buyers No. 1

The first couple, George and Melissa (not their real names), found their ideal home. It was nearly perfect. They asked their Realtor many questions, and the answers often raised more questions. They had a hard time resolving the questions and answers because of unresolved issues in their own lives. They struggled to get that first offer on paper. It took weeks. They had many insecurities from their past that hindered their ability to move forward with their plans. While they knew consciously that they could trust their Realtor, subconsciously they could not seem to move on her advice. They battled internally with nearly every decision along the way, with great emotional turmoil, and ultimately they made an offer only to turn it down at the contract signing. Their perfect home became doubt that the living room was a tad bit too small. Their decision angered the seller who put off all other offers for their offer, and today they live with regrets. (They never knew there was anything like the psychology of buying a home.)

The Psychology of Buying a Home – Buyer No. 2

The second buyer, Stephen a (not his real name), also found his ideal home. It was nearly perfect. They asked their Realtor questions, comprehended his answers and made wise decisions that were in his best interest. By the way, he also hired a mature and experienced Realtor who he knew he could trust absolutely. Joe was emotionally and psychologically mature, so he did not have uncontrollable emotional switches, and he did not engage in subconscious self-sabotage. He promptly made a reasonable offer on a home he needed in the town (Mastic Beach) that he had envisioned, and after one counter offer, they reached mutual acceptance. Their transaction closed smoothly, and they lived happily ever after. (This couple internalized the lessons of a psychology of buying a home, but they never analyzed it as such.)

The Psychology of Buying a Home

These two stories are true stories. Not made up. In fact, these two stories repeat themselves in real life over and over again. I have personally witnessed these two patterns many times over the past decades. Which buyer will you choose to be? George and Melissa or Joe?

There is such a thing as the psychology of buying a home. If your Realtor is unaware of this, or the importance of understanding how to interpret the seller's behavior during the negotiations and due diligence period, you may not end up moving into the home of your dreams. But if you and your Realtor understand the psychology of buying a home, and can work through all the issues that come up, you just may be one of the lucky buyers who buy the dream home, and live happily ever after without regrets.

CREDIT

Now unlike other real estate brokers, I am going to begin with not explaining the home buying process but beginning with your credit. Yes, I said it! Credit is a major decision maker in the housing industry and should be evaluated, organized and corrected before getting on to the home search.

What Is Your Credit Score?

First-time home buyers should obtain a copy of their credit report and review it. Your mortgage company will pull your credit, but it helps if you know before you start the process. There are places, like Quizzle.com and creditkarma.com where you can actually get a free credit report. If you find an error, it's much easier to fix it before a house has been found, rather than dealing with it when trying to close on the loan. Your mortgage banker can even give you tips to help with any minor blemishes. But why wait til you have laid your eyes on the house of your dreams only to find out that you cannot make an offer and another buyer gets your house.

The 3 national credit reporting agencies in the United States are Equifax, Experian, and Trans Union. Experian was formerly known as TRW.

You can contact the 3 national credit reporting agencies directly at:

Equifax	TransUnion	Experian
P.O. Box 740241	P.O. Box 1000	P.O. Box 2002
Atlanta, GA 30374	Chester, PA 19022	Allen, TX 75013
1-800-685-1111	1-800-888-4213	1-888-397-3742

These national credit agencies are for-profit companies owned by their shareholders. They are not government entities or funded by the government. The 3 national credit reporting agencies are competitors of each other, and they do not normally share their credit information except in special cases. That is why it is important to order a credit report from all three. I repeat, they do not share their credit information and it's up to you to make sure all of them have the same information.

Credit agencies or bureaus gather their consumer credit information by soliciting creditors such as credit card companies, banks, and lenders to join their systems and contribute their credit experience on consumers to the systems. In return for submitting information to the systems, creditor members may use the system to obtain credit information on consumers to approve credit decisions or review existing consumer accounts.

Credit agencies are generally regulated by the Fair Credit Reporting Act (FCRA), which is the Federal law generally covering consumer reporting agencies including credit reporting in this country. Individual states may also have their own versions of the law. Under Federal law credit reporting companies known as CRAs (consumer reporting agencies) have numerous responsibilities to protect consumers and their credit information.

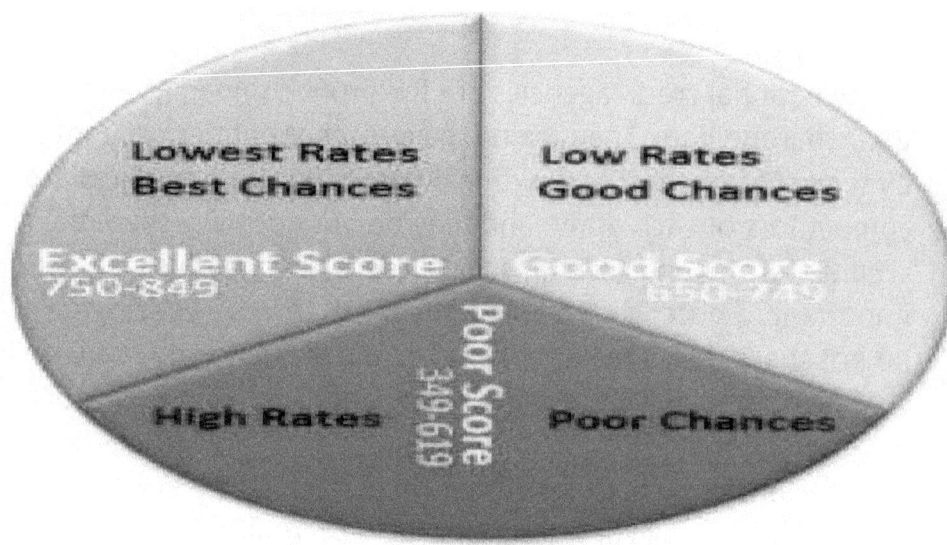

There are many people debating whether they should renew the lease on their apartment or sign a contract to purchase their first home.

Housing Cost & Net Worth

Whether you rent or buy, you have a monthly housing cost.

As a buyer, you are paying *YOUR* mortgage.

Every mortgage payment is a form of what *Harvard University's Joint Center for Housing Studies* calls *"forced savings."*

"Since many people have trouble saving and have to make a housing payment one way or the other, owning a home can overcome people's tendency to defer savings to another day."

The principal portion of your mortgage payment helps build your net worth through building the equity you have in your home.

As a renter, you are paying *YOUR LANDLORD'S* mortgage.

Below is an example of the home equity that would be accrued over the course of the next four years if you were to buy a home by the end of this year; based on the **results of the** *Home Price Expectation Survey*.

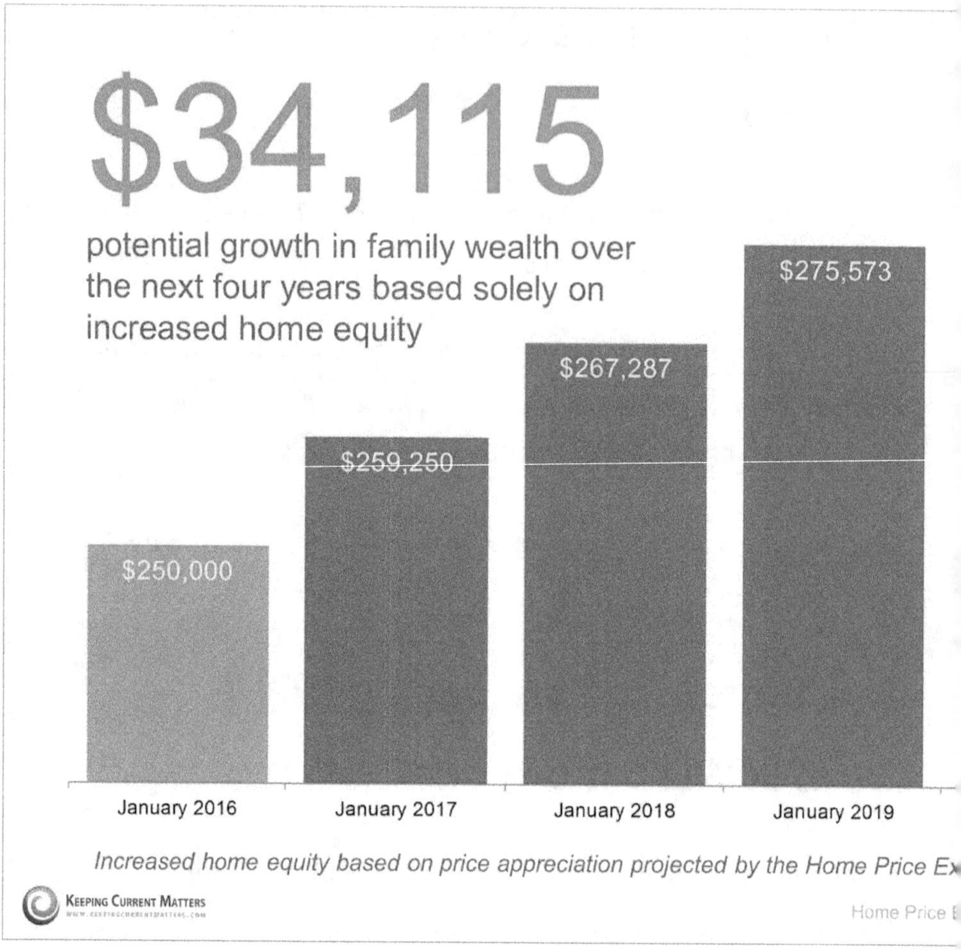

$34,115

potential growth in family wealth over the next four years based solely on increased home equity

$275,573

$267,287

$259,250

$250,000

January 2016   January 2017   January 2018   January 2019

Increased home equity based on price appreciation projected by the Home Price Ex

KEEPING CURRENT MATTERS
WWW.KEEPINGCURRENTMATTERS.COM

Home Price

In this example, simply by paying your mortgage, you have just increased your net worth by over $34,000!

Bottom Line

Use your monthly housing cost to your advantage! Meet with a local real estate professional who can explain the opportunities available in your market.

Down Payment

When you get a mortgage to buy a home, lenders require that you make an upfront investment, which is called a down payment. A typical down payment ranges from 5% to 20% of the purchase price.

For instance, let's say you find a great place and negotiate with the seller to buy their home for $300,000. If a lender approves you for a loan with 10% down, you'd have to pay $30,000 ($300,000 x 10%) plus additional closing costs, out of pocket and borrow the balance of $270,000.

So, the amount of down payment money you need to save depends on 2 factors: the purchase price of the home you buy and the percentage required by the lender to pay upfront. The larger your down payment, the smaller your mortgage and monthly payments will be.

A huge benefit of paying at least 20% down is that you don't have to pay private mortgage insurance (PMI). This is an additional monthly expense you must pay which protects the lender in case you default or don't make payments as agreed. However, you can cancel PMI if you pay down your mortgage so you have at least 20% equity in your home.

For these reasons, paying 20% down is the gold standard. But for many people, coming up with that much money is about as easy as running an ultramarathon in the desert. My advice is not to let the 20% rule keep you from becoming a homeowner if you find an affordable property that will be a good long-term investment.

Let's straighten it out. Odds are, if you're reading this, you may be thinking it's time to finally start looking for your first house. But before you dive in, it's important to get your finances organized and know what you can afford. Let me give you some information to get you moving toward this major purchase.

Pay down your debt. And while you're at it, check your credit score and look over your credit report. This is just a reminder of what I told you in the beginning! If you don't have a good credit score, you may not get the best interest rate. In fact, you may not get a loan, period.

So before you do anything else – long before you do anything else – focus on paying down your credit cards, paying your bills on time and raising your credit score. (A score of 720 and above is generally considered good, and 750 to 850 is excellent). You want your future mortgage lender to like what it sees when it comes time to request a loan for a house.

How Much

Home Can You Afford?

As you start planning to buy a home, begin with the end in mind. Be realistic about the average home prices where you want to live.

Research home listings online at realtor.com or speak with a local real estate professional. Then contact several lenders to ask about their mortgage requirements so you'll know what to expect when the time is right to make a purchase offer.

How much home you can afford depends on several factors, such as your income and expenses, credit rating, down payment, and the going interest rate for mortgages. A common rule of thumb is that your monthly housing expense shouldn't exceed 25% to 28% of your gross income.

Also, consider how becoming a homeowner fits into your overall financial goals, such as saving for retirement or a child's education. Never buy a home if the monthly payments would leave you strapped and unable to provide for your financial future.

Key Questions you should Ask Yourself before Getting the Keys

There are the key questions you, as a first-time home buyer, should ask yourself. Lets go through them and take notes on what you come up with. This is a learning process and the way we learn is to remember, some of us lose our learning (bad memories) so right it down.

How Much Home Can You Afford?

As a first-time home buyer, it's important to have an accurate idea of how much money you can borrow for your new home and most importantly, how much you can afford. Sometimes those two aren't exactly the same (depending on your financial situation), so always use what you can afford as your main metric for deciding how much house you should mortgage. One of the realities of first-time home buying is the frustration of finding that perfect home only to discover that it is not in your price range. Finding out how much home you can afford is actually not that difficult. Your mortgage banker will help you, of course, but first you can try using purchase calculator that can be found online with any bank or even told to you by a real estate agent.

Pre-Qualified or Pre-Approved?

Some many of my clients come to me asking, "Should I get a pre-qualification or a pre-approval? This can confusing to first-time home buyers, who think they will qualify for a certain amount. But in actuality, not at all! All the information has to be verified.

With a pre-qualification, no information about your finances is verified. You might find out later that the amount you were "pre-qualified" for is far different than what you actually WILL qualify for (or even afford).

What you need is a "pre-approval" in which more information (your credit and other factors) are checked and you can have a better idea how much you can afford for your first home. With a pre-approval, you're in a better position to negotiate because the seller knows that your offer is more solid. Getting this done with a loan officer in the beginning will avoid wasting time looking at homes outside your price range or even looking at houses too soon.

What Kind of Mortgages Should

You Consider? For first-time home buyers,

mortgages can be confusing and a bit overwhelming. Ask your mortgage banker every question you can think of. There are no dumb mortgage questions, especially for first-time home buyers. A good mortgage banker will ask you numerous questions about your specific financial needs so that they can match you with the best mortgage. The mortgage best for you will depend on your current financial situation if your income is steady or fluctuating. We will go through the types of loans to consider.

First-Time Home Buyers Loans insured by the Federal

Housing Authority (FHA) are designed to help everyone realize the dream of owning a home. And they're ideal for first-time home buyers! Because the FHA insures these mortgages, FHA lenders can work with borrowers who've had credit problems, collections, past bankruptcy filings, or debt-to-income ratios that are higher than normally allowed.

Applying for an FHA loan

The Interview with the loan officer
On the phone Q & A , the specialist will discuss with you where you are right now and help you determine your best way forward. If you don't pre-qualify right away, your specialist will suggest ways to improve your profile, so that you may become eligible in the future.

Within 10 minutes, you'll usually know if you're ready for a mortgage. The interview is also a great chance to get acquainted with your specialist, who will play an important role in your becoming a homeowner. Good communication with your will increase your chances of a successful and speedy process!

What paperwork will I need? Start gathering
paperwork. Not everything about buying a house involves
calculating numbers. You'll also want to start looking at
paperwork with numbers on it. Yep, the fun never ends.

So start gathering your federal income tax records for the past
couple of years, recent paycheck stubs, canceled checks for rent
or utility bill payments and any other paperwork a mortgage
lender might want to see, like credit card and student loan
information. Processing a mortgage involves gathering
documents to verify information. Assembling all of the
documentation that you may need which may include (but is not
limited to) W-2 forms, two-weeks of pay stubs, credit reports, and
bank statements. After your approval, you'll receive a
pre-qualification that includes a checklist specific to your file. This
checklist will itemize all of the things you must submit before
receiving a commitment.

- W-2 forms
- two-weeks of pay stubs
- credit reports
- bank statements
- other asset statements

Choosing the Right House for the Right Price

What Is a Reasonable Offer?

Unless you are very familiar with your area and completely understand how to price an offer on your first home, you might want to consider getting help from an expert. A real estate agent can be very helpful in deciding how much your offer should be. In today's buyer's market, your best reasonable offer might actually be lower than you would think. Have your real estate agent run comparable sales in your area and pay attention to prices per square foot for recent sales. This can give you a very good idea of how much to offer.

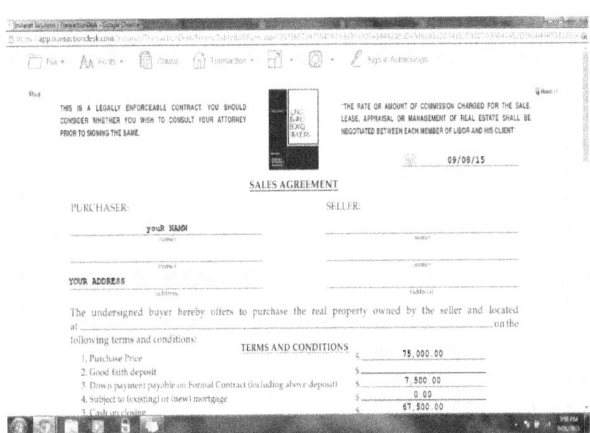

Signing your Purchase Agreement

The purchase agreement sets the amount of your offer and usually includes extra details, such as which appliances stay, who pays closing costs (seller can pay closing costs on some home loans) and when you'd like to take possession of the house. The seller (or selling agent) will have you sign the purchase agreement and offer "earnest money." Earnest money is a deposit showing that you're serious about your offer to buy the home; it's usually three percent of the asking price and later applied as part of your down payment or other closing costs. It is a check that your agent holds on to until the offer has been accepted.

*If you choose not to work with a realtor, seek the advice of an attorney to help you prepare your documents.

Should You Have the Home Inspected? Yes,

you should. You should never buy a home without inspecting it, and most purchase agreements are contingent upon inspection. Spend a few hundred dollars and hire a qualified/licensed professional to inspect your new home (before you buy it) —it's the only real way to ensure the home is in good condition. The home inspector should provide a very detailed summary report listing the condition of each item, and recommending repairs. You should always be there when the home inspection takes place. It usually takes a few hours and you'll learn not only about the condition of the house but how everything works. Ask questions as you go along. If there are problems, the seller may adjust the purchase price of the home or simply repair the problems. There's always the possibility that the home is in such bad shape or has some monumentally costly problem that it's no longer the home you want. If that's the case, get your deposit back and resume your house hunting. These are the cases when you'll be most happy you got an inspection.

The Inspection A thorough inspection includes:

Heating and cooling systems
Plumbing and electrical systems
Structural integrity of walls, floors, ceilings

foundation
roof Condition of gutters, spouts
insulation and ventilation
major appliances, garage, etc.

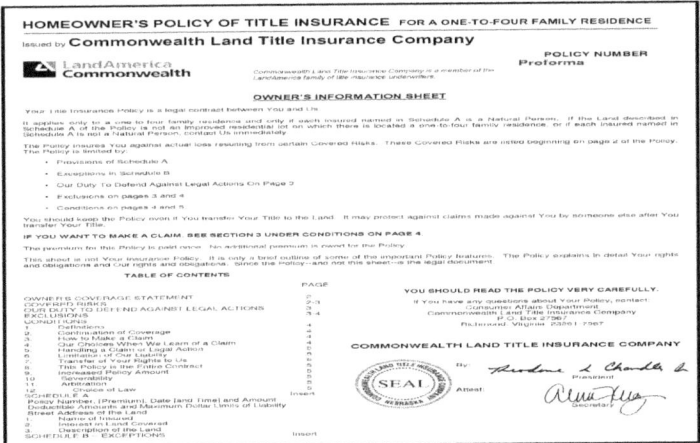

Do You Need Homeowner's Insurance?

Yes, you'll need a valid homeowner's insurance policy before you close on your home. You can't get a mortgage without it.

What Are Closing Costs?

This is probably the top asked question by first-time home buyers. All mortgage lenders are required by law to disclose in writing your estimated closing costs and fees, so you'll know ahead of time. If you don't get this from your mortgage lender, you know something is wrong. Back out before you waste any money.

This estimate is commonly called a "good faith estimate." Keep in mind, various additional costs might apply depending on your state, mortgage type, and down payment amount.

Before your closing, you'll receive a document that outlines the actual costs you'll pay at closing. You'll be asked to bring a valid picture ID, a certified check (if applicable) for any down payment due (or you may have to wire the money to the title company) and any other additional documents that your circumstances may require.

Be sure to ask for and to take a final walk through of the property shortly before the closing to make sure the home is in the condition you expect it to be.

Who will attend the closing—you, your lender, the seller, respective attorneys, the real estate agent, the transfer agent (if it's a co-op), the managing agent (if it's a condo) and the title company representative. Once everyone signs the appropriate documents and the checks are exchanged, you'll be given the keys to your home and that's it!

So there you are! As a first-time home buyer, you're on your way to being better prepared for getting a mortgage and buying your first home. Don't take chances!

Should I have money in the bank? Yes, have money in the bank. Most experts suggest that you have at least 20 percent of the house's purchase price saved as a down payment. You can certainly buy a house without that – and many people do – but there are plenty of good reason to put down at least 20 percent.

1. For starters, you'll almost certainly avoid paying private mortgage insurance, or you won't have to pay it for long. PMI is typically 1 to 2 percent of the value of the loan, split into monthly payments. It may not seem like much, but if it adds, say, $100 to your monthly mortgage payment, you can see why you'd like to avoid it.
   $20,000 in a bank account, and you're thinking of buying a house in the not-so distant future, hang onto it. This isn't the time to buy that feel good toy or emotional purchases.

2. Fine-tune your budget. Regardless of what you have in the bank now, this is a long-term, year-after-year, month-after-month expense you're going to take on. Let's see how much you can afford to spend? The mortgage, interest, property taxes, homeowner association fees, expected costs to moving, utilities, amenities that you're going to have to take care of, a pool?? You need to plan for much more than by asking yourself if you can afford the mortgage.

3. First, know your budget or set a monthly budget that you will be comfortable with paying that will not put you under a difficult strain should you not be able to work for several months.

   That might sound a little harsh, but think about it. If this is going to be a house you'll live in for years, there are going to be good and bad times ahead. You want to be prepared.

4. Think about how you'll pay for the house. Yes, with money. But **will you take out a fixed-rate mortgage or an adjustable-rate mortgage?** Adjustable Rate Mortgages- ARMs had a terrible reputation after the Great Recession, and for good reason. With an adjustable-rate mortgage, you'll get the lowest rate available – but then it will adjust after several years, often based on an index, like the Cost of Funds Index. The main point here is that your payment with an adjustable-rate mortgage won't stay the same.

   But the interest rate for an ARM is low, and if you believe you aren't going to live in your house for long, it might be a good fit for you. Some ARMs also have a limit on how much they can adjust, which may make them more appealing.

*First-time home buyers also may not know mortgage brokers are paid a higher commission for an ARM than on a fixed-guaranteed loan.

Consider the length of your home loan. Most homeowners go with a 30-year mortgage. Others try for a 15-year loan or somewhere in between.

The immediate benefit of a 15-year loan is that it's a shorter-term loan, and you typically get a much lower rate than a 30-year loan,

If you can do a 15-year loan, it's a no-brainer that you'll spend less on your house than you will with a 30-year-loan, but plenty of people can't swing that. The payment will be higher, and you need to make sure you're comfortable with the higher payment.

Scout out where you want to live. It isn't enough to think you want to live in a certain geographical area, like the west side or north side. You really need to narrow it down.

*Many neighborhoods are different and change from one block to another, so the purchaser should be aware of what their money will get in their favorite neighborhood.

Tax rates will be different in different communities, of course, so that's another consideration. There are some neighborhoods you may not be able to afford, so it's good to get a sense of that early on to avoid experiencing a huge letdown. Of course, you can wait until after a lender approves you for a mortgage, and you may want to wait until you've found a real estate agent to show you the ropes.

But once you truly know you can afford to buy a house, driving around a neighborhood will start to make the idea of home buying real – and besides, it'll provide you with a much-needed break with a more enjoyable set of numbers: **street numbers**. It's far more fun imagining yourself living somewhere than envisioning how you'll pay for it.

What happens after I make an offer?

I found that most buyers don't know what happens during this process so let's go through it step by step.

There is usually a deadline is usually given to the seller when you place a written offer on a house, it is part of the offer documents you signed. Your real estate agent should be able to tell you how long the seller was given to give you a response.

Three things will happen after an offer is made:

1. The seller accepts your offer as is

2. The seller counters your offer with specific terms

3. The seller rejects your offer (which can be done in writing or simply by not replying).

You wait for the acceptance of your offer, rejection of your offer, or get a counter-offer in return. Depending on what was written in the purchase offer, this typically happens within 3 days.

Ask the Realtor (that's me) helping you with the purchase for guidance on the buying process.

How do you chose a lawyer or an attorney?

How do you choose the best lawyer for your needs? Legal services are like any other product: the wise consumer conducts thorough research before making an informed decision. Once you secure several lawyer referrals with expertise in the appropriate practice area, you should carefully research each candidate. Even though we as realtors may suggest lawyer or attorneys remember that you are hiring them and you must feel that they know how to proceed effectively on your behalf and you both get along. Below are five steps to choosing the best lawyer for your legal needs.

1. Conduct candidate interviews. One of the best ways to assess a lawyer's legal ability is by interviewing the lawyer. Most attorneys will provide an initial consultation (usually an hour or less) at no charge. A few important questions to ask during this meeting are:

1. What experience does the lawyer have in your type of legal.
2. How do you choose the best lawyer for your needs?
    ○ Legal services are like any other product: the wise consumer conducts thorough research before making an informed decision. Once you secure several lawyer referrals with expertise in the appropriate practice area, you should carefully research each candidate .
3. How long has he been in practice?
4. What is his track record of success?
5. What percentage of his caseload is dedicated to handling your type of legal problem?
6. Does he have any special skills or certifications?
7. What are her/his fees and how are they structured?
8. Who else would be working on your case and what are their rates?
9. Does she/he outsource any key legal tasks for functions?
10. What additional costs may be involved in addition to lawyer fees (postage, filing fees, copy fees, etc.)?
11. How often will you be billed?
12. Can he provide references from other clients?
13. Does he have a written fee agreement or representation agreement?

14. How will he inform you of developments in your case?

Keep in mind that a higher fee does not necessarily equate with a more qualified attorney. Also, a rock bottom fee may signal problems, inexperience or incompetency.

After meeting with the lawyer, you should ask yourself the following questions:

> Is the lawyer's experience and background compatible with your legal needs?
>
> Did he provide prompt and courteous responses to your questions?
>
> Is he someone with whom you would be comfortable working?
>
> Are you confident he possesses the skills and experience to handle your case?
>
> Are you comfortable with the fees and how they are structured?
>
> Are you comfortable with the terms of the fee agreement and/or representation agreement?

You can always search the attorney through NYS Bar Association to be at ease. It also includes lawyer and law firm ratings based upon peer reviews which may help when choosing between two equally qualified candidates.

2. Ask other attorneys. Lawyers know the skill and reputation of other lawyers. Attorneys may be able to provide information about a fellow lawyer that you may not find in a book or online

such as information about a lawyer's ethics, competence level, demeanor, practice habits and reputation.

 *You should always check references, especially if you located the attorney through the Internet. You can also check a lawyer's peer review ratings online. Peer review ratings provide an objective indicator of a lawyer's ethical standards and professional ability, generated from evaluations of lawyers by other members of the bar and the judiciary in the United States and Canada.

3. Tour the lawyer's law office. You can tell a lot about an attorney from his law office. Request a brief tour of his office, beyond the office or conference room where you met with the lawyer. Is the law office neat, orderly, efficient and well-run? What kind of support staff does the lawyer employ? Does staff appear friendly and helpful? Is the lawyer's office local and easily accessible? Is a large portion of his office space unoccupied? Watch for red flags such as mass disarray, unhappy staff members, empty offices and unreturned phone calls.

The $$ Can I get down payment and closing assistance?

Before I purchased my first house, was approached by the director of housing within the program I was on (Section 8)to be part of a year long program that would match what I saved to go towards my down payment, if I wanted to buy. Well, if you know me, I hope right on that program, completed all the pre-requisites and gained my check for my down payment. I also searched around and spoke to people in the industry only to find there are a number of programs available.

Special Programs for Homebuyers

Many federal, state and local agencies administer programs to assist people who need help buying a home. Some of these are loan programs; others provide assistance with down payments or with building a home.

Federal Housing Administration (FHA) mortgage loans
U.S. Department of Housing and Urban Development (HUD)
451 7th Street S.W., Washington, DC 20410
Telephone: (202) 708-1112
TTY: (202) 708-1455

These mortgages, administered by the U.S. Department of Housing and Urban Development (HUD), are government-insured loans that offer very low down payments, which may be borrowed from relatives. Rates are often lower, and qualifying is easier because credit is not as large a factor. These loans are often assumable, meaning you can take them over from the previous owners or allow a buyer to take it over from you. Refinancing is easier, and there are other products and services available. There is, however, a cap on how much can be borrowed. Processing may take longer and appraisal guidelines may be strict; the house must be worth the selling price. FHA mortgages are not restricted to first-time borrowers.

U.S. Department of Veterans Affairs (VA) Home Loan Guaranty Service

VA mortgages are government-guaranteed loans available to veterans of the armed services, those currently on active duty or in the reserves, and widows or widowers of veterans. Like FHA loans, VA loans have guidelines that allow more people to qualify. In addition, some VA loans require no down payment at all. There are limits on the size of VA loans, but usually they are large enough to cover the purchase of moderately priced homes across the country. VA-guaranteed home loans are made by private lenders. The guaranty means that VA will protect the lender against loss if the veteran or a later owner fails to repay the loan.

U.S. Department of Agriculture Rural Development Housing & Community Facilities program

This program provides a variety of financing for low- and very-low income buyers in rural areas. If you are a farmer or live in a rural area, ask mortgage lenders if you may qualify. The Rural Housing Service (RHS) provides a number of homeownership opportunities to rural Americans, as well as programs for home renovation and repair. RHS also makes financing available to elderly, disabled, or low-income rural residents of multi-unit housing buildings to ensure they are able to make rent payments.

The American Dream Downpayment Assistance Initiative

authorizes up to $200 million annually around the country for downpayment assistance. To be eligible for ADDI assistance, individuals must be first-time home buyers interested in purchasing single family housing. A first-time homebuyer is defined as an individual and his or her spouse who have not owned a home during the three-year period prior to the purchase of a home with ADDI assistance. ADDI funds may be used to purchase one- to four- family housing, condominium unit, cooperative unit, or manufactured housing. Individuals who qualify for ADDI assistance must have incomes not exceeding 80 percent of area median income. ADDI provides funds to all states and to local participating jurisdictions that have a population of at least 150,000.

American Dream Downpayment Assistance Initiative (ADDI)
American Dream Down Payment Assistance
362 Gulf Breeze Pkwy Suite 313
Gulf Breeze, Fl 32561

Federal Housing Assistance Programs

Long Island Housing Partnership, Inc. was created to address the need for and to provide affordable housing opportunities on Long Island for those who are unable to afford homes, through development, technical assistance, mortgage counseling, homebuyer education and lending programs. Prospective homebuyers who meet maximum annual income restrictions and qualify for private mortgage financing are selected by lottery or computerized random number generating systems, and then on a first come first serve basis, if additional applicants can be accommodated.

Long Island Housing Partnership
Phone: 631-435-4710
Fax: 631-435-4751
Email: info@lihp.org
180 Oser Avenue
Hauppauge, NY 11788

Teacher Next Door program HUD designed this
program to encourage teachers to buy homes in low- to moderate-income areas. Those who work full time for a public school, private school, or federal, state, county or city educational agency as a state-certified, classroom teacher or administrator in

grades K-12 may qualify. You must be in good standing with your employer.

Your employer must certify that you are a full-time teacher or school administrator. You don't have to be a first-time home buyer to participate. However, you cannot own any other home at the time you close on your home. You must agree to live in the HUD home as your only residence for three years after you move into it.

Habitat for Humanity International is a

nonprofit, nondenominational Christian housing organization that helps low-income people build and buy houses. Three factors make the houses affordable to low-income people worldwide.

The First Home Club is a grant program in New York

State that provides down payment and closing cost assistance to first-time homebuyers who meet income eligibility guidelines. This grant program through the Federal Home Loan Bank of New York matches four dollars for every dollar you save up to a maximum assistance grant of $7,500. Borrowers must save $1875 of their own funds to maximize the matching funds grant.** Learn more about eligibility and how to participate in the First Home Club.

An M&T Loan Officer can assist in determining if you are

qualified and enroll you in the program. Once qualified, you will receive a First Home Club Referral Authorization Form to open a First Home Club savings account and get started.

I'm still waiting to close!! What's taking so long now? <u>What is a title Search?</u>

The purpose of the title search is:
- To verify the seller's right to transfer ownership.
- To discover any claims, errors, assessments, debts or other restrictions on the property.
-

The title companies find and fix problems with the title in 25% of transactions-usually without the the borrower or lender even knowing it! In addition, title companies pay millions of dollars each year in claims. Title insurance provides significant value to lenders and homeowners.

Before closing, the title company searches the public records for all matters affecting title. The search entails examining the records in the offices of the Register of Deeds, Clerk of Courts, and other municipal and county officials. These records include recorded documents, judgments, liens, taxes, street easements, sewer assessments, special taxes and other matters that could affect property ownership.

Through careful examination of these records, we determine who owns the property and what interests may already exist in that property.
This process, called a title search, provides early warnings of title flaws that must be dealt with before the property can be sold or refinanced.

The Day before….. The Keys

What to look for during the Final walkthrough Before Closing on a House? When the home buying process is nearly complete, many buyers start relaxing and focusing on other details, such as purchasing new furniture and looking at paint samples. But there is one more crucial step to take before closing on the house: a final walkthrough. This is the last chance before closing. When the home buying process is nearly complete, many buyers start relaxing and focusing on other details, such as purchasing new furniture and looking at paint samples.

But there is one more crucial step to take before closing on the house: a final walkthrough. This is the last chance before closing to make sure everything is in working condition. A final walkthrough can not only help you feel more confident about your purchase and avoid buyer's remorse, it can also pinpoint any last-minute problems that should be taken care of before settlement.

When to Schedule a Walkthrough?
A house walkthrough should take roughly 30 minutes to complete, enough time for you to be extremely thorough. During this assessment, you should check for new issues that may have come up since the last time you viewed the home.

This is especially important if a major event, like a severe storm, occurred during that time period. Once you close on the home, previous owners are not obligated to fix new damages that may have occurred.

Be sure to schedule a timely walk through, about 24 hours before closing on a home, to address any potential problems.

What to Look For? At this time, you should check all major appliances to ensure they are in working condition. For example, consider turning on the dishwasher and washing machine, checking outlets and light switches and testing other basic operations. You might also request warranties and owner's' manuals for appliances.

Look to see whether any fixtures the seller agreed to leave behind (a chandelier, for instance) are missing. Check to make sure any previously agreed-upon repairs have been made. Then, look over the general condition of the property, inside and out:

1. Are there damages like scratches, walls or floors that occurred when the homeowner moved out?
2. Did they leave unwanted furniture or other things behind?

3. Is the yard and overall property in the condition it was when you last saw the home?

Many industry professionals recommend that buyers bring a home inspector with them to seek out any problems, and to confirm that repairs were made as requested and to their satisfaction. For this kind of service, home inspectors will typically charge much less than their original inspection costs.

Take Action Fast!
If you do identify problems, you have a few options. First, you may choose to walk away from the deal altogether. However, most professionals encourage buyers to consider how significant the problem is before walking away. Is avoiding a $500 fix worth losing your dream home?

In other cases, you may choose to postpone the closing until the sellers fix the problem. If sellers balk at having the problem fixed, and the repair was agreed upon during negotiations, you do have legal recourse — although it may be a good idea for the buyers and sellers to try to reach an amicable agreement to make the closing go more smoothly.

Take your time during a final walkthrough to ensure there are no surprises after the closing. Once this important last step is complete, take a deep breath, relax and smile: You are about to be the proud owner of a new home!

The Closing.... Coming to an End.

What Is a Closing?

Simply put, a closing is the final performance of all of the agreements you made with the seller and your lender for the purchase and financing of your new home. If you are buying solely with your own cash, no lender will be involved. If you are financing your purchase, however your loan will close at the same time and place as your purchase.

A closing is often called "settlement" because you — as buyer -- along with your lender and the seller are "settling up" among yourselves and all of the other parties who have provided services or documents to the transaction.

Settlement involves the simultaneous exchange of documents, and funds required to complete the transaction. You pay the purchase price to the seller with a combination of your down payment, your own funds, and the proceeds of your loan. In exchange, the seller gives you a deed and other transfer documents, and clear title to the property.

You receive the proceeds of your loan from your lender — the face amount of the loan less fees and initial interest. In exchange, you give your lender a written promise to repay the face amount of the loan, and a lien on the property. The seller pays off the old loan and pays commissions to the real estate agents (per the listing agreement between the seller and the listing agent). Both buyer and seller pay their respective fees and costs to the various parties who contributed funds, services, or documents to the closing.

Exercise your writing hand, and bring your favorite pen to the closing, because you will be signing a lot of documents.

What and Where Your Closing Will Take Place

If you are taking out a loan, your closing will take place at the office of a settlement agent, also called an "escrowee." The escrowee can be the title company — that is, the company that insures your ownership of the property. However, in some states (such as Alaska), or local areas (such as Southern California), you are more likely to close at the lender's office, or at an escrow company. Upon request, some title or escrow companies will send a mobile escrowee to close in a location convenient to all of the parties.

If you are purchasing your home for cash, no lender is involved, so you and the seller can decide the most convenient closing location. Your attorney, or the seller's attorney, may offer his or her office, but restrictions in client trust accounting may make it impossible for the attorney to disburse funds immediately.

Some closings are "witness-only." That means that a notary or attorney goes to a location convenient to the buyer and seller to provide the loan documents and disbursement services. However, the notary or attorney will not explain the legal effect of the documents or the closing. Witness-only closings are not legal in all states. For example, Connecticut, Delaware, and Georgia require an attorney to complete all aspects of the closing. These closings will often close in the attorney's office.

The time leading up to your home purchase closing is going to be busy. You'll be cleaning, packing, contacting movers, changing over your utilities, and deciding which of your household items to move, sell, or give away. If you're moving to a new community, you'll also be changing your medical and other professional service providers, registering your children in new schools, and finding a new health club, grocery store, or favorite restaurant. With so much to do, it's often difficult to focus on the details of the closing.

You may have hired an attorney to negotiate your purchase contract and help you through the closing process. If so, your attorney will help explain the closing process, review the closing documents, calculate the funds you need to bring to closing, and notify you of what items you should bring. Your loan officer or mortgage broker can answer your questions about what you need to do to meet any outstanding loan conditions. Your sales agent will schedule your walk-through, and can contact the listing agent if you have questions for the seller.

Unfortunately, much of the information you need to complete your closing will come at the last minute, just when you'd prefer to focus on your move. That's why this article may come in handy, to help you understand the big picture: what a closing is, and what will happen during the closing. For details on the documents that will be created or exchanged at the closing.

At last, most likely several weeks after your offer to buy a home was accepted by the seller, you are preparing for the closing day. This involves you paying for the property, the lender (assuming you have one) funding your loan for a portion of that payment, and the seller transferring title. But the most time-consuming part of the closing involves your reviewing and/or signing the various documents required to bring this about.

Real Estate Transfer Documents

Most of the documents related to transfer of ownership of the property must be signed by the seller and delivered to you, the buyer. It's important to review these for accuracy and completeness. With many state and local variations, the main purchase documents in your home purchase are likely to include:

- **The deed.** This document transfers the property from the seller to the buyer. State law dictates its form and language, but you can choose the form of ownership in which you take title: individually, in trust, in joint tenancy or in other tenancies. The deed is given to the county recorder of deeds to record, and made public. Recording your deed puts you in the property's chain of title so that anyone looking at the county records can see that you took your title from the prior rightful owner, and therefore, own the property.

- **The bill of sale.** This transfers all of the personal property that is being sold along with the house, such as furnaces, air conditioners, appliances, light fixtures, window treatments, security systems, antenna, or cable or dish TV equipment, from the seller to the buyer. The document will typically list the property to be transferred, or refer to the contract that lists the personal property.

- **The affidavit of title or seller's affidavit.** Although the actual name of this document varies by state, it is a sworn, notarized statement by the seller confirming ownership of the property and describing any known title defects such as leases, liens, or work on the property that could potentially create liens, boundary line disputes, or outstanding contracts for the sale of the property.

- **Transfer tax declarations.** Many states, counties, and municipal governments charge real property transfer taxes and require the buyer and seller to sign declarations disclosing the purchase price and calculating the tax.

Home Loan Documents

The loan documents are prepared by your lender or a servicing agent for your lender. How many documents you have to sign and what's in them will depend on the lender and the type of loan you chose. The typical loan documents are:

- **The note.** This provides evidence of your debt to the lender, a description of the loan terms, and a means for the lender to transfer or collect the debt. It will state the amount of the debt, the initial interest rate, the terms of any interest rate changes, and the time and place that you must repay what you owe. The note has value in and of itself, just like a check or money order. If your lender sells your loan (as is common), it will physically give the note to the loan purchaser.

- **The mortgage.** The mortgage is your agreement to put up the property as collateral for the loan. It is recorded, along with the deed, in the county recorder's office, and becomes a lien against the property — meaning that the lender owns an interest in your property up to the amount outstanding on the loan at any given time. In literal terms, the lender can foreclose upon and sell the property if you fail to repay the loan or otherwise comply with its terms.

- **Loan application.** You completed a loan application form when you first applied for the loan. The lender will type a new form with the information that you gave in the original application for the closing, and ask you to review it for accuracy and sign it. If your financial position has changed since your original application -- for example, you have lost your job or taken on another credit card or debt -- you must inform the lender before signing.

- **Loan Estimate and Closing Disclosure.** For those who apply for a mortgage on or after October 3, 2015, two new forms, called a "Loan Estimate" and a "Closing Disclosure," replace the HUD-1 Settlement Statement, the Good Faith Estimate, and the Truth-in-Lending disclosure form that were formerly required in mortgage loan closings. These forms are designed to help you better understand the mortgage loan transaction.

Various other disclosures and agreements may be included in the loan package. In the compliance agreement, you agree to cooperate if the lender needs to fix any mistakes in the loan documents. IRS forms W-9 and 4506 allow your lender to report your mortgage interest and obtain copies of your tax returns. Servicing disclosures tell you if the lender is going to use a servicer to collect your payments, or whether the lender intends to sell your loan to another lender or an investor, and where to send your payments. Tax and insurance escrow forms allow the lender to charge and hold fund to pay real property taxes and insurance premiums on your behalf.

The lender may also ask you to sign affidavits certifying that you are going to occupy the home as your primary residence, and confirming your legal name and any other name you may use on accounts and legal documents.

Real Estate Title Documents

Just when you think you are finished reviewing and signing documents, the title company and escrowee will give you their documents.

The main title document is the title insurance commitment (the "Commitment") showing the party in title (who owns the house), hopefully the seller. It will also show all of the liens or other clouds on title. If you have one, your attorney will review the Commitment to make sure that title is in the condition promised in the contract and otherwise acceptable under local law and custom. If you are relying on an escrow company, it will review the Commitment to make sure title complies with the conditions stated in the escrow instructions created to satisfy the lender's requirements. If title is not acceptable, the seller may have to pay off additional liens, or obtain additional signatures. Unexpected title issues could halt or delay your closing.

CAUTION: Some title issues can be very complex. If your seller does not have an attorney, or if local custom dictates, you may have to do more to ensure title will be good in time for the closing. If neither party has an attorney, you may wish to contact the title company well prior to the closing to obtain the Commitment, and review it with a title underwriter.

Still Signing The title company will ask you to sign its customary closing documents. This will include an ALTA statement, which is a one-page affidavit very similar to the seller's affidavit of title; a judgment affidavit, where you list your recent judgments, divorces, or bankruptcies; a compliance agreement, in which you agree to cooperate with the title company to correct any closing mistakes; and a disbursement agreement, allowing the title company, as escrowee, to disburse the loan proceeds. There may be additional disclosures informing you that an attorney is involved in the transaction, or that the lender has an affiliated businesses arrangement with the title company, or that the loan title insurance policy will not cover your interest as the buyer. And that is why you should be advised by your attorney and or your real estate professional to obtain a homeowner's insurance policy.

When the Closing Is Over

When all the above is done, you become the owner of the property. You will be allowed to take possession immediately or shortly after the closing, unless you have made an agreement with the seller to take possession either earlier or later. All of the requirements, tasks, and other promises in your contract with the seller will be met, completed, or delivered, unless you have made post-closing agreements. Common post-closing agreements involve reimbursements for real property taxes when the exact amounts to be due are unknown at the closing, or repairs that could not be made prior to the closing.

It might be the most nerve-wracking, **empowering yet most difficult life choice you will make but when you decide it's a road worth traveling.** I hope you'll find all the information helpful and educational because I have found just knowing something bolsters your self-esteem, and more. I have made every attempt to give you the life's experience but its up to you to maintain that information. Now I am not telling you to go out to ask everyone and their mother about buying a house, because everyone has their own spin on things. Use my motto, "if it's not professional information, it's just opinion."

If this has assisted you please share it or direct others to Amazon to purchase this book. I would love for your to post your review, comments and suggestions on the Amazon link for this book.

If you are planning an event, training program or conference and are interested in hiring Edna J. White to speak or deliver a training course please contact him at 631-772-9098 or by **msedna12@gmail.com.**

www.ingramcontent.com/pod-product-compliance
Lightning Source LLC
Chambersburg PA
CBHW070335190526
45169CB00005B/1898